POEMS OF SELF WONDER AND SCIENCE

Rhythm of Life Philosophical Verse

by
Joseph A Mercado

Library of Congress Control Number (LCCN): 2026908685

ISBNs:
eBook: 979-8-90224-253-6
Paperback: 979-8-90224-254-3
Hardback: 979-8-90224-255-0

Published by:
Authors Publishing House
1178 Broadway, 3rd Floor
New York, NY 10001, USA

Main Line: (855) 624-0155
Email: support@authorspublishinghouse.com

josephamercado47@gmail.com

Table of Contents

Dedication

This book is lovingly dedicated to my mother, **Elizabeth Thalia Burgos Mercado (1932–1992)**, whose guidance in speech and grammar, along with her unwavering belief in me, laid the foundation for who I am today.

It is also dedicated to my brother, **Victor Manuel Burgos (1969–2025), in memoriam**, whose constant encouragement and enduring faith in my abilities continue to inspire me. His words reminding me that I could achieve anything I set my mind to will always remain with me.

Acknowledgement

I would like to express my deepest gratitude to my wife, Jeanette, for her unwavering support throughout this journey. Her constant encouragement, insightful discussions on poetry, and willingness to listen as I read my work aloud have been invaluable. I am especially thankful for her thoughtful feedback and inspiration, which have greatly contributed to this collection.

Introduction

Poems of Self Wonder and Science explorations of who we are, how we relate and use our creativity to communicate our feelings and understandings. Looking through scientific and poetic lenses.

Life involves Poetry and Science, that keeps our inquisitiveness 'otherwise known as curiosity' alive. That guides us with self wonder. I have learned that science and poetry compliment each other. Seeking meaning in our selves and the world we live in.

After all these years teaching science with a dab of poetry, while observing, thinking and seeking nature's questions through living life. I am grateful to continue on this journey of life's winding roads and travels.

Thank you for choosing this highway to accompany me. I hope that you find something that speaks to your creative self. Maybe, you never know. You'll want to write some poetry about how you feel, how you see things, what's going on and express yourself.

Cross Roads and Destinations

The Teacher

Hey look over there,
It's the Teacher,
The Teacher.

I didn't know what I wanted to be.
It's always been there in me.
Yea, in me.

A teacher wanting to come out and be free.
Be free of the everlasting reality.

Hey look over there,
It's the teacher,
The teacher.

To teach human beings
The complexities of life.
To fight for your right.

To make a choice.
To speak in a loud voice.

Hey look over there,
It's the teacher,
The teacher.

I can feel it, you know what i mean.
To fill the cracks, to fill the seam.
To maintain that foundation beam.

It must be the others in me.
The fisherman,
The philosopher,
Don't you see?

Hey look over there,
It's the teacher,
The teacher.

I see a reflection,
Just for your inspection.
Come on, reach out,
And make the connection.

You Think School

You think school is not cool,
But it's the best learning tool.

So don't be a fool,
Be cool
And stay in school.

Hang out with your best friend,
Don't let the good times end.

Listen to me everybody
Listen to me.
Come closer;
Hear what I got to say.

You think you got it made in the shade.
But think again, peer pressure
Will get you every time.

Education should be a live inspiration.
Down with perspiration.

Chill out and you'll find out,
That school
Will lift you out
Of the situation.

Use your imagination,
Get an education.
Live up to the expectation.

Do your investigation,
Practice communication,
Live for the observation,
Enjoy the association.

Live the realization,
That education
Is your best
Salvation.

Right Road

You think you have it in the bag.
But you know it's really sad.

Go ahead mess up your important education.
You might as well go on vacation.

Can you make it on the street,
You think so.
Dream on
Stay incognito.
Get with the flow
Follow the beat.

Life is important
So you better regulate.
You better relate.

Don't sit around
You'll be dead weight.

Rumors gossip social life.
What's more important,

Not to fail, do good with delight.
To become educated to see the light
To be successful, oh what a sight.

Living in society and having a profession.
Supporting family use your discretion.

I know it can be stressful.
Living the life be successful.

You'll be so proud to be cool.
Having a wonderful life,
Now use the right tool.

This Is It

This is it; you can do it, go for it.
Come on, easy come, and easy go.
Take it in, analyze it,
Understand it, you know.

Knowledge is abstract and concrete.
Info is necessary for the streets.

Let's Sing.
Life is beautiful, life is real.
Life is beautiful, I can feel.

Success is what you want
Don't let anyone get in your way.
You have the final say.

Listen, listen. do the right thing.
Forget about the ching, ching.

You can always get bling, bling.
Don't want to end up in sing, sing.

Get down to business.
Study hard.
Get your butt off the floor.

Everything is at your disposal,
Do what you are supposed to.

Knowledge is everything.
Knowledge is everything.
Knowledge is everything.

Wanna Be Somebody

Stay in school, stay in school.
School is hot, school is happening.

Where else can you make friends for life.
You don't have to run the streets looking for a fight.

I'd rather be at school with my buds and friends.
Not hanging out at a scary dead end.

Study hard don't let things slide.
Get a huge slice of that apple pie.

Things will fall in place,
You might have to steal 2nd base.

Knowledge is everywhere go for it,
It's right there.
Take it in, fill up the bin.

Absorb it, relate to it, and grow with it.
I know you got it, so don't sweat it.

Permission

Someone said 'write a rap song about permission.
I guess I'm on a very important mission.

Ask for permission do the right thing.
Forget about your sparkling bling, bling.

Don't just walk out of the room.
Listen to the teacher,
Sit down watch the main feature.

Be respectful and considerate,
You come to school to be literate.

What comes around goes around?
Just pay attention, don't be a clown.

Ask for permission, it helps your relationship.
Go ahead dream about being on a gigantic
Spaceship.

You can be who ever you want,
Ask for permission, start your mission.

Take Care of Your Mind

Take care of your mind and soul to rejuvenate
Really think about it don't you hesitate

Good night's sleep, wake up fully refreshed
It's a journey ahead of you, your personal quest

Ready to go completely energized
Tackle the world head on, finalize

Choices and decisions you must make
Give your all, everything stay awake

See things from all angles and perspectives
Analyze everything to include the reflective

Down the road to your new high school
Making new memories - blend old school

Another awakening to create more neuron cells

Everywhere in your self firing connections

What a super duper spell

The Rhythm of Knowledge

Deep Earth

You can go very deep into the earth,
Probably as far as it's birth.

The deeper you go the hotter it gets.
Pressure closes around you, don't fret.

High temperatures come from the outer core,
7 thousand degrees maybe even more.

Going down through the earth' layers,
Seeing strange things you better say you're prayers.

Diamonds, diamonds the hardest thing around
Be careful exploring, stop being a clown.

Pressure increasing the more you go down,
Popping your eardrums making you frown.

Density and temperature also increase,
Better bring a big dinner so you can feast.

Rain

Rain you can't get enough of it
Can't live without it
Continous water cycle from time before time
What a hit

Water vapor combining forming liquid droplets
What a sight
Thunderous sound on the skylights
Everyday is a fight

Constant erosion great impact meandering streamlets
Rolling with brooks streams rivers into oceans,
Cycle resets

Tremendous potential energy tranforming into kinetic energy
Constructive and destuctive forces battling it out,
It's sensory

Hail rain sleet snow precipitous
Falling of changing water vapor
Slipping sliding on the slick water
Channeling the weather shaper

Vastness of the immense evaporation

Condensation watercycle

Super mist in the tropical rain forest

Trees absorbing waters life

Diversity of the species fighting for survial

Water life's energy

Adaptations evolving envormental connections

To old memory

4 billion years since beginning of continious water cycle

Intertwined into evolutionary life

Endless ways to recycle.

Plate Tectonics

Erupting volcanoes exploding very fast.
Rocks flying everywhere, coming from the past.

Shake and bake, rock and roll,
Erupting volcanoes toil and toll.

Look over the rim. what do you see?
Magna changing into lava, it's not beyond me.

Shake and bake, rock and roll,
Erupting volcanoes toil and toll.

Volcanic ash all over the place.
You better run and cover your face.

Seismic waves travel the earth,
Radiating from the epicenter
Of its birth.

Shake and bake, rock and roll,
Erupting volcanoes toil and toll

Tsunamis 100 feet high,
As it hits the beach
Everyone sighs.

The lithosphere of love is where the plates reside.
Floating on the asthenosphere bye and bye.

Shake and bake, rock and roll,
Erupting volcanoes toil and toll.

Energy of earth creates the quakes,
That rock and roll and break the plates.

You have heard the mighty phonics,
Of our world of plate tectonics.

Minerals

Minerals, minerals,

The're all around the world.
We'll try to explain,
So give it a whirl.

Calcite won't put up a fight,
So what a sight.
To see it bubble to the acid test,
Just like the rest.

Minerals, minerals
You know what they are
Use um, abuse um, reuse um.

Diamonds, diamonds
The hardest thing around.

The greeks say invincible,
I say in the ground.

Minerals, minerals
You know what they are
Use um, abuse um, reuse um.

Limestone
It's just fossil rock,
Don't look at the clock.

Chalk is used on slate board,
You can write out the chord.

Minerals, minerals
You know what they are
Use um, abuse um, reuse um.

Sulfur
Smells like rotten eggs.
Take a whiff,
Don't fall off the cliff.

It's soft and yellow,
So don't get mellow.

Minerals, minerals
You know what they are
Use um, abuse um, reuse um

Halite
Salt of the world.
Nacl, colorless and pale.
Water melts salt,
It's not your fault.

Talc, talc
Soft baby powder.
Go ahead eat your chowder.

Minerals, minerals
You know what they are
Use um, abuse um, reuse um

Pyrite
Fools gold, shiny and bright.
Don't worry it won't bite.

Apatite
Not as clear as nite.
Can be yellow, green,
Brown and white.

Minerals, minerals
You know what they are
Use um, abuse um, reuse um
25

Now you've heard my minerals rhyme.
So get on line and drop me a dime.

Moonscape

I see only one side of the moon
Everyday even in the month of june

Moonquakes occur due to meteors, gravity
Cause by temperature change - a travesty

Drifting away from earth at 3.8 cm per year
It will still be our satellite and has no atmosphere

What you weigh on the moon
Is 1/6 of your weigth on earth

Even if you're fooling around at noon
You can buy a scale at woolworth

The gravity of the moon causes ocean tides
That moves water low and high, slippery slide

Humans travel to the moon, you see rocks, dust
Maybe aliens everywhere what's the fuss

Solar eclipse moon blocks the sun
Using your special glasses having some fun

Old man on the moon is watching us all
As we all play together having a ball

The Mystery of Mealworm

A squirmy organism that moves around
When you hold it, you can act like a clown

Observe and infer record your notes
Take this multicellular on a boat

Does it make any sound
Many observations science bound

Put your ear close to it
Don't be scared or catch a fit

How many legs, how many eyes,
Use a magnying glass to be a spy

Other parts might be hard to find
Looking through a mcroscope will be fine

What does it eat, did it grow
Daily observations how do you know

Comes in many colors to be seen,
Laughing with yor friends in between

The scientific method an inquiry process
Share your results with your posse – progress.

Experimental set-up use a control
What is the variable that's the goal

Eduacational Seeds of Understanding

Tera Nova: Resource Earth

Chemicals that ruin earth are bad.
We need to be careful, i'm really sad.

Protect, don't waste resources.
We'll go back in time and use lots of horses.

Trees, air and water are renewable,
But don't let Dr. Suess fool ya.

Plastic, cans and paper can be recycled.
Go down to the landfill with your bicycle.

Omnivore, herbivore, food chain,
Help save wildlife, don't be a pain.

Tree hugger, hug that tree,
Do the right thing and be free.

Earth day, everyday, that's the time
To conserve and preserve, that will be fine.

Going Into the Wide, Wide World

Going into the wide, wide world.
You need to adapt to your new situation.
Embrace your path to a new world.
You have a new direction be part of the creation.

Lots of new learning this year.
Be proud of your accomplishments.
Go foreward without any fear.
This is your time to recognize acknowledgements.

Remember to be safe, responsible and show respect
It will come back to you, that's what to expect.

Explore your new situation with an open mind
Study very hard and you'll be fine.

You will be making new friends, creating new experiences.

Leaving middle school is another beginning, not the end.

Think about what is right

Remember that we live in a society that has high expectations.
Go for the goal of attaining many aspirations.

Things can get complicated just like a spiders web.
Take your time, figure it out instead.

The path you take is your responsibility
Be wise thinking of the possibilty.

Oasis

Study very hard, you'll go real far.

Beam me up scotie. don't forget the assessment.

Use your brain and forget about the pain.
Go ahead, look for the treasure,
It won't make you insane.

Study island is lots of fun.
We can go to the beach
And bathe in the sun.

It's progress they want to see.
So get your act together,
Become a busy bee.

Do real good and pass the assessment.
You'll graduate at commencement.

You have to do the pre and the post.
So sit down, login and do your most.

The pre-test, to see what you know.
That's your grade so don't be afraid.

Get on the boat and study hard.
Take the post-test and get paid.
35

You're sailing right along.
See the island so study strong.

This is the assessment,
Go ahead cash in your investment.

Study island, it's right there.
Go ahead growl like a bear.

Water Everywhere

Watch out for the water cycle,
Go ahead and ride your bicycle.

You need to be watchful of precipitation,
While you are going to your destination.

Going down the road, you see clouds of evaporation.
Use your brain think about your situation.

Rain, snow, hail, sleet,
Hurry up, you don't want wet feet.

Condensation occurs in the clouds,
Now you can shout-water cycle out loud.

Riding your bike, watching things grow.
Enjoy life, dance in the snow.

The water cycle is run by the sun.
When It's all over, you'll have some fun.

Round and round the water cycle goes.
It cycles here and cycles there,
So ride your bike and be aware.

Inspirational Echoes of Resilience

Symbiosis

Nature is alive today as its silence and
Sounds reverberate around the garden

Eliciting interactions between different species,
Dead dragonflies harden

A wonderous view of scent and bees buzzing around blooming flowers
reflecting in deep thought sitting and meditating about life's power

Listening and observing the details of germinating seeds into sprouts
bringing together the beauty of symbiosis of plants and animals, no
doubt

Watching birds chasing each other and foraging on the earth's
bountifulness.
Life's resilience continues to follow nature's purpose and
beautifulness

Sitting here quietly on a windless sunny day in reverie and reflecting
about the fragile balance of life and the continued resilience of nature.

At First Your Brain

At first - you're brain, think for yourself
As you write ideas show you're real self

Creativity will flower and blossom
You can play dead like a possum

Use your knowledge from deep within
The hippocampus of the brain

Where memory is stored, it's a win, win
Practice! practice! will help you reign

Stop asking others for the answers
Critical thinking is for dancers

Remember! remember! to brainstorm
Bring out the knowledge show your form

Happy Birthday

A new life, another starting!
The arising of another you, all new.
Believe it, happy birthday.

A new creation. The release of a new self
Out of the ashes of the old.

The reproduction of the self.
A brand new start into the
Reality of the now.

Yesterday, forever gone.
But today believable beyond
Tomorrows imaginations.

Oh! birthdays, the celebration of a new birth
Of the soul. a rekindling of beliefs into the
future.

A roller coaster ride into the dreams of a
New birthday. The casting off of the old shell,
The awareness of another new you.

An exposure of vibrant energy,
The energy of anticipation.

The wonderment of a newborns excitement,
Integration into a conscious dream of bliss
And happiness.

Nothing But a Wanabe Rapper

Nothing but a wanabe rapper.
Dreaming all my life,
To be a magnificent beat mapper.

Starring into the lookin glass.
Watching as everything
Catches up to me real fast.

Fantasizing about life in the fast lane.
What a life that could be,
What about the pain.

Waking up to the reality of now.

Don't let it pass you buy.
Rise up to the occasion,
Go ahead and fly.

Fly away to the dreams of tommorow,
Forget about the possibility of sorrow.

Go back to the crystal ball.
See your future, it's written on the wall.

Waking up to the reality of now.

I can see it now, all around me.
Can't you see it, it's gonna be reality.

See it for yourself.
Go ahead and dream.
Dream of being a rapper,
A beat mapper.

Stay In School

Stay in school get good grades
Learn for real and then get paid.

Teachers care they care a lot.
Learn to trust don't be a fart.

If you did it take the blame.
Grow up to be a good citizen,
Don't be a shame.
It's all about the numbers,
It's not a blame game.

What It comes to, is life is for real.
Get off your high horse don't make a big deal.

Still in code did you figure it out.
Better think hard, don't you doubt.

You feeling it, i'm feeling it.

Importance of it all
I could only emphasize.
Do you hear the call?

You feeling it I'm feeling it.

Breaking inspiration down
Into nothingness.
I said to my son just for fun.

He said how's it my fault,
I just walked through the door.

Teach Lessons Beyond Books

Oh Deer

Oh deer you wild thing
In my organic apple orchard
Surviving off the land
In the forest and on the meadows.

Mother caring for her growing fawn
Eating the luscious food of the garden.

Early in the morning I saw both of you,
Fawn running into the woods
Mother in the orchard eating apples.

I stopped to look at your beauty
And you frooze, you were gone
When i came back.

The fence was supposed to protect,
But instead the delicious apples
Enticed you to take a step foreword
To enjoy and sustain.

I Was Born to Rap

I was born to rap,
But I'm an old man
What you think of that.

Rapping away at the school,
Teaching science to the lab stool.

I want to learn, learn,
I want to teach, preach,
I want you to reach for the stars,
Start with your feet.

Listen, listen, what did you hear.
You hear kids laughing.
It's not at the beach;
It's not in the streets.
Yea, it's in the classroom,
Where you have the right beats.

Discipline is what you want to relate to.
I don't mean behavior,
Oh no
It's not the savior.
But you know what to do.

Osmosis, it's the prognoses.
Absorb it right thru the membrane.
Your quite right it might make you insane.

Knowledge,
That's what you want.
Just as is, raw unchanged.
Think about it;
Swish it around
In your amazing brain.

You think this rhytme is dope,
I tell you it's not,
And it's full of hope.
Hope to be free,
To live in this immense society.

To show everybody
That you have what it takes,
To relate to all the possiblity.

Yea, yea, the old man is right.
You need to fight for education.
Because that's what will get you
Your individual emancipation.

Peering thru the looking glass,
You know you want to pass.
Pass thru to the next grade,
Come on,
Don't be afraid
Go for it,
Go out and get paid.

Success that's what's relevant,
Get off your wild horse
And forget about the elephant.

Race down to the reality of life,
You know what that means
Keep up the good fight.

Yea, I was born to rap,
But I'm an old man
What you think of that.

In The Bag

You think you have it in the bag.
But you know
It's really sad.

Go ahead
Mess up your education.
You might
As well go on vacation.

Can you make it on the street,
You think so.
Dream on, stay incognito.
Get with the flow
Follow the beat.

Life is important
So you better regulate.
You better relate.
Don't sit around
You'll be dead weight.

Rumors gossip social life.
What's more important,
Not to fail,
Do good with delight.

To become educated
To see the light
To be successful
Oh what a sight.

Living in society,
Having a profession.
Supporting family
Use your discretion.

I Know it can be stressful.
Living the life
Be successful.

You'll be so proud to be cool.
Having a wonderful life,
Now use the right tool.

Yo Teach

Yo teach you don't need to preach.
All I wana do is hang out at the beach.

Don't talk to me about school,
I'll have a better time swimming in the pool.

I'm telling you forget the beach.
Forget the pool.

School has everything you need,
For the family you have to feed.

Hey teach,

I remember the day at the school yard.

You came by to philosophize
About life and everything.

I took your advice and through away the dice.

I knew you could make it
You didn't have to fake it.

Success is what you want.
Education is the font.
The more you get the more you want.

Yo teach,

Thanks a lot for taking the time,
Now i know that i will be fine.

Be bold go for the gold.

You'll end up at the top

With your body and soul.

Beat

You know it will be a feat,
When you give me a great beat.

Running down town
Stomping your feet.
Come on. you can do it,
Don't be cheap.

Dig deep into your sub-conscious mind.
Before i collect a $500 fine.

Quick, quick read the sign.
You know what it says,
Rap on a dime.

Let it rip. we'll get it later,
Back on the flip...side that is.

See what i'm getting at,
You have the beat inside you.

Bring it out,
You know what its all about.
Use the mic and let it all out.

Rap away
Use your heart beat as a tick-tock.
Rhyme with your ipod,
Put it in the dock.

Get the right music,
But don't you lose it.

Rapping with the music.
That's what its all about.
Go ahead give it a shout.

Reflections

Reflective

Relating to deep thought
Being self thoughtful
Thinking about things

Because I think about things that happen in the pass,
Present and what could happen in the future.

I want to remember about friends, family happening's.
I want to maintain relationships, create new experiences
To reflect about.

Reflection happens all the
Time with the conscious and
Unconscious mind.

We do it while awake in reality
And sleeping during dreaming time.

Going back in time to relive an experience
Try to remember, feel it and be serious.

Connections follow and become part of you.
In the present relationships evolve into a view.

A view that is constantly changing into a deeper
Understanting of the bonds we develop and
The love we have for one another.

Think! School!

School staff
You must think fast.
Have a good time,
Have a blast.

You're on your feet,
Teaching these kid's.
It's really great,
You know what you did.

You're at a big meet.
That's a huge feat.

Busting your butt
Meeting deadlines.
Being careful,
Watching out for fines.

That's what it takes
To be at the top of your game.
See the reality, accept the pain.

*We know
We got it going on,
We're the best
And really strong.*

*Don't let anybody tell you otherwise.
A tremendous praise,
We deserve a huge pay raise.*

*We're ahead of the rest,
So be advised.
Whatever it takes,
Don't be surprised.*

*It's unscripted.
Don't be mystified.
It's encrypted.
I survived.
I'm alive.
Wanna testify.*

*We work hard.
But it's worth it.
You gotta work it, work it.*

Progress that's the main goal,
Stick with the program
Stay in the foal.

Life is an ever changing scene.
Think about it,
You know what i mean.

You can smile,
You deserve it.
It's been a while.

Teaching isn't it great.
You have an impact.
Now that's a fact.
So keep it straight
And relate.

Life

Life is amazing! life is beautiful, wonderful
And spectacular all at the same time.

Now is the time to look deep within yourself
And at the relationships you have created.

There is nothing more meaningful than living beings.
But you must do the right thing.

You need to take care of yourself and go forward,
Not just for anyone but for yourself.

No one is going to do it for you more than you can do
For yourself. You must take advantage of every good
Opportunity that comes your way.

Make lots of friends
Show that you are a beautiful person,
And have a very dynamic personality.

It is a very difficult road for us all to travel,
But you might as well have a good time doing so.

Nothing is impossible for you to do.
You can do anything you really want to do.
Go for it, have a wonderful life.

Time Travel

Sitting here at my computer trying to create music,
Thinking about life.
Slideshow flashing through my brain.
Endless flashes of the past -phantasmorgoria.

Listening to a beat,
What a feat - multi-tasking!
Something is lost,
Lost to alternate space and time.
Can you get it back - rewind.

Make decisions, always seeing the whole picture
Encompassing all reality.
Flashes of future possibilites.
Take this - no take that path.

What the heck flip a coin.
Heads or tails,
It's that way - fast.
Seeing is believing,
Faith is what you need.
You need it fast.

In a rocketship, what a blast.
Into the worm hole you go
Don't blink - you're in the past.

Someone comes into the room, distracts you.
Your thought is lost. whos the boss.
Get it back, get it back.
There it is, that's a fact.

Universe permeates in the self
And out into the beyond.
Ring, ring, it's the phone.
What do you thnk,
Let it ring, let it sing.
Trying to reflect.
Thoughts to collect.

Yo! Yo, come here, listen to this.
Need somebody to hear what i got to say.
Something you don't want to miss.
Share,

That's what you gotta do.
Inner thoughts for you, don't be a fool.
Deeper, deeper into the self.
Don't get loss,

You'll never find you way back.
Bread crumps of reality,
Leave a trail, hold on tight.
follow it back to the now.

Light at the end of the tunnel,
Squeezing yourself into the contracting funnel.
Just in time to see your other self wave.
Until next time, i'll be fine.

Blink! blink,

Shaking myself out of reverie.

Oh,

What an experience, next query.

Ever Expanding Universe

What do you think about the big bang?
Go ahead and drink your tang.

Collect your data and observation, action reaction - no hesitation.

Compressed, hot and dense mass, galaxies go by very fast.

Theorize for just a fraction.
Tremendous expolsion, lots of action.

Matter and energy is now here.
Where it never was don't dispair.

The ever expanding universe.
Think about it in reverse.

Expanding universe within an instant.
Don't look for anything non-existent

Every where you go there's plasma soup,
Don't be fooled don't get dupped.

Space and time is so infinite,
Is this theory really legitimate...?

Cosmic background radiation,
Watch out for our civilization.

Microwave particles document universal chronicles.

Theoretical hypothesis,
Supernova binary synthesis.